Dung Beetle Learning

Are you struggling to keep your children entertained? Or do you secretly pine to craft?

Dung Beetle is here, with a set of 20 toys and games, that can be made from corrupting everyday objects.

SUSTAINABLE
All these pieces are designed to fall apart so you can keep on crafting forever. There is no danger of becoming skilled. This is known as **sustainability** - within days, and with minimal use, they will return to Mother Nature.

RECYCLE
A list of materials is found on every page, that are retrievable from any household dustbin, to which your 'crafts' can be returned on completion.

If you manage to actually make anything, send your finished craft to studio@dungbeetlebooks.com for a chance to win a unique, sustainable gift.

THE DUNG BEETLE PLAY AND
LEARN SCHEME

Things to make and do

In a cost of living crisis

Written by M ELIA
Illustrated by M ELIA & R PHILP

PUBLISHED BY
Dung Beetle Ltd © 2023
Created in a salubrious East End ghetto

SOCIAL MEDIA BUBBLE

This small plastic stress ball can be used as a comfort blanket.
Every time you find yourself confronted by an alternative point of view, online or in real life, give it a squeeze. Your social bubble pal will fulfil the fantasy of everyone agreeing with you on everything all the time.

YOU WILL NEED:
Bubble wrap
Yellow and white card
A marker pen
Double-sided sticky tape
Cling film

1. Take the bubble wrap, scrunch it up into a big ball and secure with sticky tape.

2. Draw your favourite emojis and write affirmative messages on speech bubbles - remember, don't write anything that might make you reconsider your position.

3. Stick them on to the bubble wrap ball, then cover in cling film.

4. Grasp tightly when in conversation with an adversary.

QUICK FIX BOTOX FOR MUMMY

Being an old woman is rightly a criminal offence.

However, you can make your mummy look ten years younger, with this homemade plasticine Botox filler.

She will be elated with her new look, and may eventually develop the confidence to inject real plasticine into her face and leave the house.

YOU WILL NEED:

A recent picture of your Mummy (or Granny).
Plasticine
A pretty frame for presentation

1. Take the picture and apply the plasticine over all wrinkles and unsightly features.

2. Fill out lips until they are disproportionately large.

3. Remount in a gold frame. Your improved mummy (or granny) is now worth it.

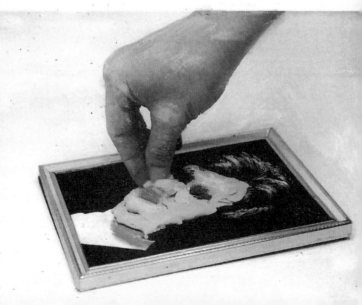

EQUALITY RACE

This racing game provides a speedy solution to the 'competetive spirit.' Effort and talent can have no impact on outcome, as all three contestants are joined hand and foot.

This is the perfect appliance to crush a prodigious child.

YOU WILL NEED:

The lid from a shoebox *A piece of balsa wood*
Screws *Corks*
Matchboxes *Diversity of paint*
A screwdriver
A knife for cutting (ask a grown-up for help)

1. Take the old shoebox lid and cut 3 sections out of the top and one out of the side (as shown).

2. Insert 3 screws into the piece of balsa wood in line with the cut sections, then insert 3 corks onto the screws.

3. Paint in different colours (obligatory).

4. Cut 3 gold matchboxes in half and glue onto shoebox to make first places for all on podium.

DOOM SCROLLER

Remind yourself to be **permanently afraid** with this rotating headline tin can. Apply the latest media alerts to your customary staples (e.g. climate change, celebrity paedophiles, and drag-queen story time.) Curate and scroll while you wait to be boiled to death within 5 years.

YOU WILL NEED:

An empty coffee tin
2 panel pins
Some wire
A cork
Horror porn

8 Lolly sticks
A Hammer
Pliers
Glue

1. To make your Doom Scroller take the tin and make a hole in the centre of each end.

2. Collage the digitally enhanced horror porn from the paper of your choice.

3. Bend a piece of wire round in the shape of a handle (as shown). Insert wire through the tin and glue at each end. Put a cork on the end of the handle.

4. Hammer panel pins into lolly sticks to make trestles.

5. Position on desk. Scroll for 5-6 hours a day, to help you through your digital detox.

THE COMMUNICATOR
Great old-fashioned fun for kids.

Bring the paper cup and string phone up to date, by smashing a nail through at least two tablets.

Practise 'talking' and 'listening.'

Beware of shards of broken glass.

YOU WILL NEED:
2 broken tablets
2 large nails
Hammer
Some string

1. To make your Communicator, hammer a nail into two broken tablets or smart phones. Tie a piece of string from one nail to the other nail.

2. Speak and listen, whilst standing not very far away from each other.

3. With any tablet you can scream into the void.

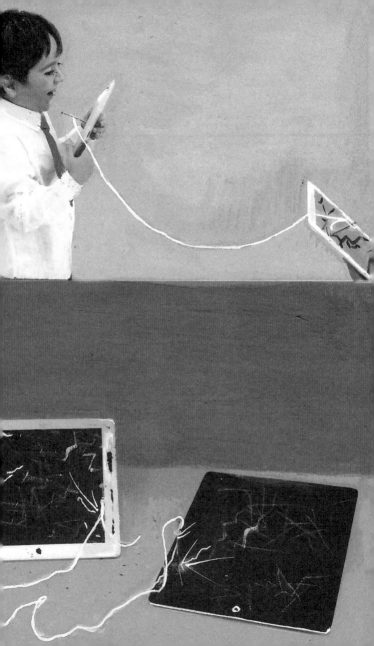

SEXUALISED HOUSEHOLD OBJECTS

A trendy way of vamping up household rubbish, is to relentlessly sexualise it.

A tin can, egg box or fairy liquid bottle can be magically transformed into a *desirable* celebrity, with secret mental health problems.

YOU WILL NEED:
> *Household objects of your choice*
> *Paint*
> *False eyelashes*
> *Jelly lip sweets*
> *Glue*

1. Take the household objects and paint them in the current desirable skin tone.
2. Stick on eyelashes and lip sweets.
3. Swoon in adoration.

CARBON BIG FOOT SHOES

These carbon footprint shoes will physically slow your child down, making them aware of the damage they do by walking, breathing and farting in the world.

Decorate with their favourite methane emitting animals and other rubbish.

YOU WILL NEED:

Two rectangular cardboard boxes
Images of pollutants from magazines/ internet
Glue
Scissors or a craft knife
Long black laces or string

1. Take the two cardboard boxes and cut leg-sized holes in the tops.

2. Find misery everywhere and glue on shoes.

3. Make eight holes in the top of each shoe for laces.

4. Let your child hobble through the guilt.

THE VIRTUE SIGNALLING HALO OF LIGHT

Broadcast to the world what an exceptional person you are by creating your own halo. If you haven't done anything good, so much the better: superficial is always in fashion.

Update your virtue card each time you apply lip gloss.

YOU WILL NEED:

An Alice band
Gold paint / spray paint
Card for virtuous frame
Cable ties
Gold tissue paper
Glue

1. Wrap cable ties around Alice band. Cut to different lengths and spray gold.

2. Scrunch up tissue paper to make roses then glue on to sides.

3. Make a frame out of cardboard, paint gold, then glue in the centre of Alice band.

4. Create cards with different virtues that you can display in the centre.

BROKEN EGGSHELL CORPORATE MOBILE

This easy-to-make mobilc is perfect for suspending over a baby's cot. As it rotates, it will slowly and systematically attach your infant to the the global corporate behemoth of the day.

YOU WILL NEED:
A wire coat-hanger
Eggshell halves (10)
A needle or pin
Paints
Your favourite corporate logos
String

1. Carefully make a small hole in the top of each eggshell with the needle or pin.

2. Paint the eggshells with your favourite corporate logos.

3. String them up.

BRUTALIST TEDDY BEAR

Trade in your soft cuddly 'safe' bear for this stark, utilitarian teddy.

Place far away from children to encourage their blossoming nihilism and emotional detachment.

YOU WILL NEED:
Old polystyrene packaging
Grey spray paint
Black paint
A junior hacksaw

1. Hack up polystyrene into desired shape.

2. Spray paint the surface of the polystyrene grey. It will erode the surface a little, this is a good thing.

3. Paint the teddy bear's face on with the black paint. Make sure he looks very serious.

PRIVILEGE MASK

Find out if privilege is real, with this authentic old school 'white man' mask.

Access the highest echelons of society and the swankiest restaurants in town.

If you can't cover your bill, remove for a hassle free escape on the night bus.

YOU WILL NEED:
An empty cereal box   *Cotton wool*
Elastic   *Pinkish Paint*
Glue
A knife for cutting

1. Cut back and bottom off the cereal box with craft knife. Then cut out shapes for the eyes and mouth.

2. Paint the whole box in a nice pink flesh tone.

3. Stick on cotton wool for the hair, eyebrows and moustache to complete the look.

4. Make holes at the side and thread elastic through.

5. Wear with your cleanest trainers and head to town.

SELFIESCOPE

Why bother looking at the world from a different angle, when you can look at yourself for long periods of time? These angled mirrors are ingeniously positioned to reveal the only person that matters in modern society - you.

Warning: Constant use required to maintain functioning levels of narcissism.

YOU WILL NEED:
> *Some cardboard*
> *Two small mirrors*
> *Sticky tape*
> *A craft knife or scissors*

1. On a piece of cardboard, draw out the measurements opposite and cut out the shape, scoring along the folds.

2. Tape the cardboard together and the mirrors on the end.

3. Look inside. It looks like you're watching the outside world while you admire your own face.

TAB

2″ 2″ 2″ 2″

7″ 10″ 8″

45° 45°

HOME-MADE METAVERSE

Disappear your child with this immersive experience that transports them to another place.

A cardboard box, images from a travel catalogue and a squirt of tropical atomiser, will keep them trapped in this escape unit.

Warning: Cut air holes, to limit risk of suffocation.

YOU WILL NEED:
A cardboard box
A craft knife
Glue
Generic travel brochure images.

1. Stick exotic locations inside the box and place on your child's head. Immerse in the metaverse.

2. Now there is no need to waste money on holidays.

OFFENCE-O-METER

Prove how aggressively offended you are
with this portable feelings thermometer.
Adjust to top temperatures to eliminate any
adversary.
Remember to be truly inclusive you have to
exclude.

YOU WILL NEED:

A cardboard box   *Transparent cellophane*
Old newspapers   *A craft knife*
Glue   *Sticky tape*
A stapler   *A hole punch*
Ribbon or string

1. Cut out shapes (as shown) from
cardboard.
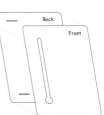
2. Cut out piece of cellophane double
the length between slots plus an inch.
3. Thread through the slots, then join
together with tape. Staple a piece of
cardboard over join to use as a lever.
4. While the lever is at the bottom, colour the front half of
the cellophane red.
4. Staple the 2 pieces of cardboard together.
5. Cut out letters from the old newspapers.
6. Make 2 holes at the top and thread through ribbon.
7. Hang offence-o-meter around your neck and look to be
offended.

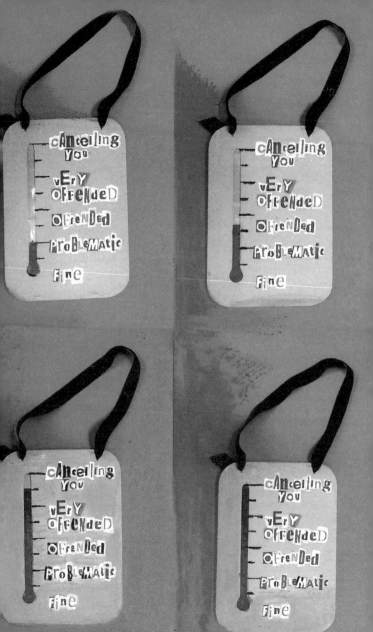

DOLL'S BEDSIT

Set your child's standards low, by encouraging them to play with this rentable bedsit. Encourage a minimalist aesthetic in a shoebox to embed the single living upcycling dream. They will never be disappointed.

YOU WILL NEED:

An old shoe box   *Cardboard*
Matchboxes   *Matchsticks*
Paper straws   *Paper fasteners*
Egg boxes   *Paint*
Coloured paper   *Bubble wrap*
Glue

1. Use all the materials to make your own bedsit furniture. Be as creative as you like.

2. Experiment with different configurations of cramped.

3. If you're feeling adventurous, try and create a space for guests.

GENDER REVEALER

According to the cleverest people (scientists), there are infinite genders frolicking inside your child. How can they find them? This simple experiment will liberate them from the obvious.

YOU WILL NEED:
A sunny window
A shallow dish
Water
A mirror
White paper

1. Fill a small white dish with about 2cm of water.

2. Angle the mirror in the water and hold the paper so the reflection appears.

3. The daylight will go through the water, which acts as a prism, and then be reflected by the mirror onto the paper.

4. The light that comes out will be split, like your child's personality, and show bands of colour on the sheet of paper. Like a disco!

5. This is a spectrum. After a few minutes the rainbow should magically reveal their true identity.

SNITCHER'S INVISIBLE INK
This one's for the kids

Are your parents contradicting you? Do they have problematic views? You are never too young to snitch on them, and report their 'hate thoughts' to the database.

This secret onion ink can be read by the State, but not by granny.

YOU WILL NEED:
An onion
An old jam jar
A quill or dip pen
Some writing paper

1. Cut the onion in half and squeeze the juice into a jam jar.

2. Dip the nib of the pen into the invisible ink and record your parents' crimes and misdemeanours.

3. Post to your local council.

4. When your parents are taken away, they will never know why.

RETRO MODELS

In the olden days, the most celebrated models started out as matchsticks (e.g. Twiggy). Take a trip down retro lane by creating a variety of micro-outfits, or for a more contemporary style, sellotape all the matchsticks together.

YOU WILL NEED:
Matchsticks
Paint
Paper
Low self-esteem

1. Fashion the matchsticks as you like with the paint and paper.

2. Film on a catwalk.

TRANSPARENCY CLOAK

Consign privacy to the past, and tell the world everything about yourself, in this see-through, shower curtain cape-of-disclosure.

Reveal all your personal details and everyone else's, (home address, birth certificate, post-partum scar photographs) and shimmy down your local high street.

YOU WILL NEED:
> *An old shower curtain*
> *String*
> *Safety pins*
> *Printer*
> *Pictures of all your parents' personal data (raid their social media accounts).*

1. Thread the string through the holes in the top of the shower curtain.

2. Use safety pins to attach all private images and information.

POST-TRUTH LIE DETECTOR

How can you tell if your friends are lying in a post-truth world? Give this machine a wobble and it will instantly confirm **your truth**. The glove is sensitive to your intuition. *Got them!*

YOU WILL NEED:

An old tissue box
Cardboard
Lolly sticks
Balsa wood
Wire
Sticky tape
A black marker pen
A rubber glove

A toilet roll
Wooden skewers
Paper fasteners
A nail
Glue
A clothes peg
White paper

1. Cut cardboard discs for inside toilet roll and glue in. Make holes in centre and insert wooden skewer.
2. At end of tissue box, secure lolly stick to each side with paper fasteners. Make hole at other end of lolly sticks.
3. Position toilet roll and secure with cardboard discs.
4. Make handle.
5. Cut out slot in top of tissue box. Tape end of white paper on another skewer and wrap around. Position skewer inside tissue box. Feed paper through slot and tape to toilet roll at other end.
6. Push large nail in top of balsa and wrap wire around.
7. Secure peg at one end and rubber glove at other.
8. Use peg to hold marker pen.

Notes/ Things I found offensive